SHOW ME THE MONEY

MONEY THEN AND NOW

by Jennifer Boothroyd

Consultant: Beth Gambro
Reading Specialist, Yorkville, Illinois

Minneapolis, Minnesota

Teaching Tips

Before Reading

- Look at the cover of the book. Discuss the picture and the title.

- Ask readers to brainstorm a list of what they already know about money throughout history. What can they expect to see in the book?

- Go on a picture walk, looking through the pictures to discuss vocabulary and make predictions about the text.

During Reading

- Read for purpose. Encourage readers to think about the role money plays in their lives as they are reading.

- Ask readers to look for the details of the book. What are they learning about money in the past and present?

- If readers encounter an unknown word, ask them to look at the sounds in the word. Then, ask them to look at the rest of the page. Are there any clues to help them understand?

After Reading

- Encourage readers to pick a buddy and reread the book together.

- Ask readers to name three ways from the book that money has been used over time. Go back and find the pages that tell about these things.

- Ask readers to write or draw something they learned about money throughout the years.

Credits:
Cover and Title page, © Glevalex/Shutterstock, © hatman12/iStock, © Sonate/iStock, and © Andrey_KZ/iStock; 3, © Fer Gregory/Shutterstock; 5, © SDI Productions/iStock; 7, © Public Domain; 8, © Public Domain; 10, © PublicDomain; 11, © Klaus Vartzbed/Shutterstock; 12, © TonyBaggett/iStock; 13, © hdagli/iStock; 14, © givaga/Shutterstock; 15, © Heritage Image Partnership Ltd /Alamy; 17, © Public Domain; 18, © Sonate/iStock; 19, © Ridofranz/iStock; 21, © paulaphoto/Shutterstock; 22, © Public Domain, © Public Domain, © Steven Giles/Shutterstock, © Nataly Studio/Shutterstock, © Maurice Savage /Alamy; 23, © Vasin Lee/Shutterstock, © Jiri Hera/Shutterstock, © Farknot_Architect/iStock, © Charday Penn/iStock, © Kotomiti Okuma/Shutterstock, © Lisa F. Young/Shutterstock

Library of Congress Cataloging-in-Publication Data

Names: Boothroyd, Jennifer, 1972- author.
Title: Money then and now / Jennifer Boothroyd.
Description: Bearcub books. | Minneapolis : Bearport Publishing Company,
  2021. | Series: Show me the money | Includes bibliographical references
  and index.
Identifiers: LCCN 2021010921 (print) | LCCN 2021010922 (ebook) | ISBN
  9781647479015 (library binding) | ISBN 9781647479084 (paperback) | ISBN
  9781647479152 (ebook)
Subjects: LCSH: Money--Juvenile literature. | Finance, Personal--Juvenile
  literature.
Classification: LCC HG221.5 .B656 2021 (print) | LCC HG221.5 (ebook) |
  DDC 332.4083--dc23
LC record available at https://lccn.loc.gov/2021010921
LC ebook record available at https://lccn.loc.gov/2021010922

Copyright © 2022 Bearport Publishing Company. All rights reserved. No part of this publication may be reproduced in whole or in part, stored in any retrieval system, or transmitted in any form or by any means, electronic, mechanical, photocopying, recording, or otherwise, without written permission from the publisher.

For more information, write to Bearport Publishing, 5357 Penn Avenue South, Minneapolis, MN 55419. Printed in the United States of America.

Contents

Changing Money 4

Money Matters: Before Bills and Coins 22

Glossary 23

Index 24

Read More 24

Learn More Online 24

About the Author 24

Changing Money

You give bills and **coins** and get back a snack.

It is easy!

But money was not always like this.

A long time ago, people did not use money.

They **traded**.

People would give what they had extra of.

They would get back what they needed.

But sometimes trading was hard.

People started using things in place of **goods**.

It was the first kind of money.

This first money was not the same in all places.

Some people used shells as money.

Others used beads.

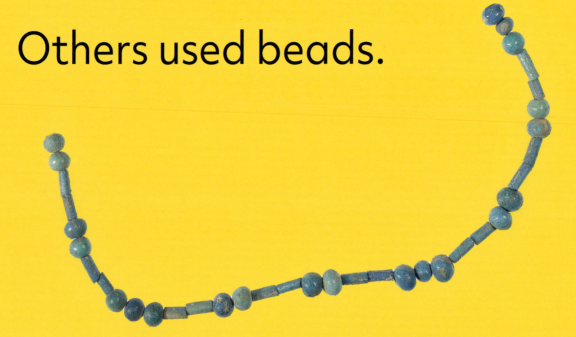

Then, people started to use coins made of **metal**.

Coins made it easier.

More people started to use money.

But big bags of coins were heavy.

They were hard to carry around.

So, people started to use paper money, too.

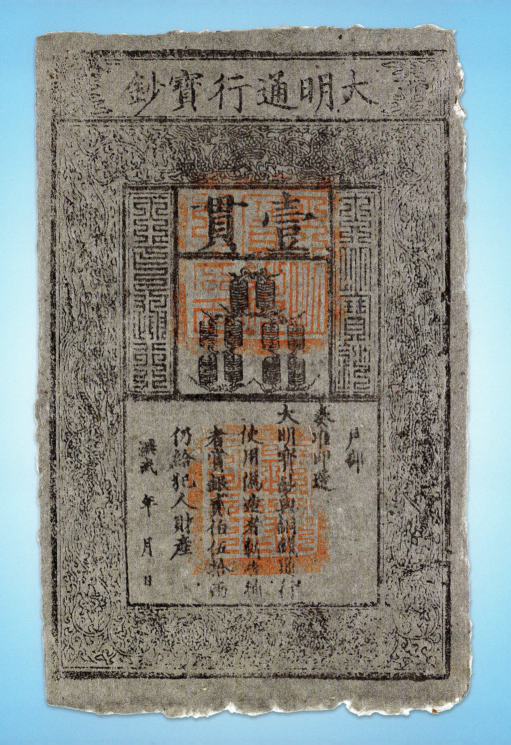

Coins and paper bills have looked different over time.

They have been different sizes.

Some have changed shape and color.

Now, there are even more ways to pay.

People can use **credit cards**.

They can use **apps** on their phones.

Money has changed a lot over the years.

What do you think it will be like next?

Money Matters Before Bills and Coins

A long time ago, people used different things as money.

- Beads
- Shells
- Stones
- Whale teeth
- Beans

22

Glossary

apps things on a phone or computer that let people do tasks

coins small pieces of metal money

credit cards cards that let people buy things and pay for them later

goods things that are made for sale

metal a hard, strong material found in the ground

traded gave one thing for another

Index

apps 18
bills 4, 16, 22
coins 4, 12, 14, 16, 22
credit cards 18

metal 12
paper 14, 16
trading 6, 9

Read More

Higgins, Nadia. *What Is Money? (Money Smarts).* Minneapolis: Jump!, Inc., 2018.

Schuh, Mari. *Money Around the World (Money and Me).* Vero Beach, FL: Rourke Educational Media, 2019.

Learn More Online

1. Go to **www.factsurfer.com**
2. Enter "**Money Then and Now**" into the search box.
3. Click on the cover of this book to see a list of websites.

About the Author

Jenny Boothroyd collects coins from places she visits.